# Akathist
# to
# Saint Irodion of Lainici

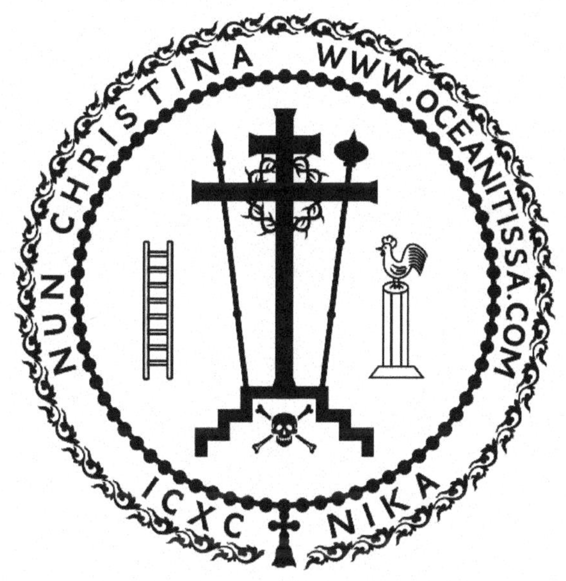


Anna Skoubourdis
Nun Christina

**Published by: Virgin Mary of Australia and Oceania 2022 ©**
oceanitissa@gmail.com
www.oceanitissa.com.au
Youtube: Nun Christina Oceanitissa

Subscribe to receive updates and Orthodox Christian creative media

www.oceanitissa.com

## May 3

### The Troparion of Saint Irodion of Lainici, Tone 5.

Let us, his disciples, glorify now our morning star from Oltenia with secret worship, as a chosen father, for Saint Irodion became a seer, healing everyone from diseases and a divine confessor.

### Troparion, Tone 1.

Spiritual Father of Saint Callinicus of Cernica, advisor of monastics and morning star of Oltenia, helper of those in need and wonderworker, oh, Holy Venerable Irodion, pray to Christ our God to save our souls.

## Akathist

### Kontakion 1

Let us all praise Irodion, the morning star from Lainici, the one with an Apostle name; for he, having become a skilled priest, the shepherd of Oltenia, showed himself to be brilliant, and in the mountain, he multiplied his disciples, who called out to him: Rejoice, Holy Father Irodion, made wise by God!

### Ikos 1

The great Hierarch Calinic of Cernica chose you as a spiritual father, Venerable Irodion, and appointed you the advisor of the monks; for, in your youth, he saw the perfection of your pious life, for which we cry out to you:

Rejoice, morning star of Lainici;
Rejoice, good shepherd;
Rejoice, for you have communed from the chalice of eternity;
Rejoice, heart of a father and maker of sons of light;
Rejoice, son of the Oltean land, received as a brother in Cernica;
Rejoice, for you have become a great abbot in the Lainici Monastery;
Rejoice, for many disciples you gave birth to in the Holy Spirit here;
Rejoice, vessel of the gift before the sight;
Rejoice, long-suffering bearer of the cross;
Rejoice, supporter of the helpless;
Rejoice, liberation by the grace of the enslaved creation;
Rejoice, word with divine fruition;
Rejoice, Holy Father Irodion, made wise by God!

### Kontakion 2

Saint Calinic often came to you for advice and release, even though you were younger than him, but your spiritual growth won with the price of sacrifice, had valued more than the long years. For this, we sing to God: Alleluia!

**Ikos 2**

Becoming a hierarch in Oltenia, God-bearer Hierarch Calinic called you, Father Irodion, to serve as abbot and named you "The morning star of the Lainici." For this, together with him, we sing to you:

Rejoice, perfection in angelic form;
Rejoice, humility of heavenly man;
Rejoice, enlightener of the faithful, the one with an apostle name;
Rejoice, friend of the Bridegroom clothed in the garment of the age to come;
Rejoice, follower of the fathers of the wilderness;
Rejoice, ornament of hieromonks with sanctity crafted;
Rejoice, earth that bears the seed of the Word hundredfold;
Rejoice, fruit of the Tree of Life;
Rejoice, secret understanding of the mysteries of Scripture;
Rejoice, pious priesthood and angelic ministry;
Rejoice, fruitful sacrifice of resurrection;
Rejoice, bright torch of our souls;
Rejoice, Holy Father Irodion, made wise by God!

**Kontakion 3**

Reverend Irodion, being received into the community of the Cernica Monastery, your abbot, Saint Calinic, marveled at your improved life, for in the labors of the monastic life, you made yourself an undefiled wedding garment, and at the Holy Liturgy, with the hosts of angels, you sang to God incessantly: Alleluia!

**Ikos 3**

The brothers ran to your monastery as at a spring of water, a great congregation thus forming Pious One, and you, Holy One, looking at them, gave thanks to God, saying: "Here I am and the infants given to me by God." Therefore, together with them, we shout:

Rejoice, trumpet of the Holy Spirit;
Rejoice, kindled candle of the unsettling light;

Rejoice, chosen vessel of the Most Holy Trinity that carries the uncontainable Word;
Rejoice, angelic life in one spirit with the Holy Hierarch Calinic;
Rejoice, deified image of the son of God;
Rejoice, for in prayer you saw the world in divine light;
Rejoice, garment of restraint pierced by the rays of the Transfiguration;
Rejoice, liturgy of the mysterious change;
Rejoice, canon of the hermits, living together with the angels;
Rejoice, Supplication of the consolation from above;
Rejoice, persistent in spiritual worship;
Rejoice, innovative building of our souls;
Rejoice, Holy Father Irodion, made wise by God!

**Kontakion 4**

Pious Saint, having the gift of foresight, you did not receive the milk of the woman who gave the wicked one the creature of God because the sacrificial offering should only be brought to God with pure love and prayer, singing: Alleluia!

**Ikos 4**

Reverend Father, you were a father of the monks, an exhortation and light to the faithful and to all who come to you faithfully. For this, by worshiping your icon and holy relics, we receive the enlightenment of mind and heart, for which we cry thus:
Rejoice, lover of spiritual tranquility;
Rejoice, unceasing supplicant to God;
Rejoice, torch of the Holy Spirit that illuminates the faithful;
Rejoice, teacher of the mysteries of Scripture;
Rejoice, herald of the Word of God;
Rejoice, pearl from the field seated in the Kingdom of Heaven;
Rejoice, foundation unbroken by the waves of the world;
Rejoice, divine peace in troubled times;
Rejoice, enlightened prophecy that encourages and edifies;
Rejoice, light of pious monks;
Rejoice, the joy of Saint Calinic of Cernica;

Rejoice, the one sanctified by the grace of the Holy Spirit;
Rejoice, Holy Father Irodion, made wise by God!

**Kontakion 5**

Reverend Father, you have become nourishing bread for the poor, father to the orphans, guidance to the lost, comfort to the poor, consolation to the sick, and God-bearing father to all, Blessed, for which you now sing unceasingly together with the heavenly hosts to the Most Holy Trinity: Alleluia!

**Ikos 5**

Humble shepherd and sweet advisor, you showed yourself in the Church of God's glory, Reverend Saint, being appointed the abbot of the monks by a call from above and placed in the chair of the primates of your lavra by the Holy Hierarch Calinic. For this, knowing that your life was like that of angels, they all rejoiced singing to you:

Rejoice, praise of Lainici Monastery;
Rejoice, glory of Oltenia;
Rejoice, body made an altar of sacrifice to the Lord;
Rejoice, lover of God and people;
Rejoice, steward of divine mysteries;
Rejoice, son of God and father of men;
Rejoice, skilled doctor of spiritual and physical diseases;
Rejoice, protector of the helpless and comforter of the poor;
Rejoice, tree with bright fruit of salvation;
Rejoice, heavenly man and earthly angel;
Rejoice, safe path to eternal joy;
Rejoice, for your prayer has become a ladder from earth to heaven;
Rejoice, Holy Father Irodion, made wise by God!

**Kontakion 6**

Saint Irodion, you became a great defender of those oppressed by unclean spirits, for through prayers, you drove away the devils with just your word and untied those caught in their nets with your blessing. For this, knowing the power of your prayers, we also sing to God: Alleluia!

**Ikos 6**

Receiving blessing and advice from you, on the way to the episcopal seat of Râmnic, the Holy Hierarch Calinic has foreseen the death of abbot Nicandru. Although saddened by the separation, he rejoiced for he had you as a gentle helper, for which we sing to you together with him:

Rejoice, strength of the hierarchs;
Rejoice, redeemer of sinners;
Rejoice, sapling of the Kingdom of Heaven;
Rejoice, chosen creation of earth and light;
Rejoice, man of divine desires;
Rejoice, holy hermit who draws people to the love of Christ;
Rejoice, for you have always united prayer with breath;
Rejoice, parental greeting of the prodigal son;
Rejoice, heart in prayer in which God rests;
Rejoice, for your soul and heart have been engulfed by unspeakable light;
Rejoice, for through the cross you brought forth the flower of incorruption;
Rejoice, beloved son of the Mother of God;
Rejoice, Holy Father Irodion, made wise by God!

**Kontakion 7**

Reverend Father, the Mother of God enlightened you and guided you throughout your life, for you brought everything under her Protection and, reaching the measure of the Fathers of old, you sang together with God's Saint: Alleluia!

**Ikos 7**

Saint Herodion, Father, serving now in the heaven's Chruch and worthily living together with Saint Calinic in the unsettling light, we fervently beseech you to intercede with the heavenly Father for our souls so that we may find mercy and grace in the time of judgment, and sing to you:

Rejoice, raising of the fallen;
Rejoice, strengthening of the weak in faith;
Rejoice, pillar of fire and bright cloud on the path of salvation;
Rejoice, weapon against evil spirits in the hermit life;
Rejoice, enlightenment of those darkened by passions;
Rejoice, cleansing of those sunk in sins;
Rejoice, bearer of mysterious gifts;
Rejoice, for you pour divine gifts over the creation;
Rejoice, harbor for the salvation of the faithful;
Rejoice, fruitful olive tree that has mercy on those who call you for help;
Rejoice, heaven of virtues, and guide to the Kingdom of Heaven;
Rejoice, safe path of those who work with humility;
Rejoice, Holy Father Irodion, made wise by God!

**Kontakion 8**

Mysteriously, the prophet David received the divine law through vigils and fasting, and communing us with the Body and Blood of Christ the Savior, you, Reverend Irodion, received the prophetic gift of the Spirit, for which you sang to God: Alleluia!

**Ikos 8**

Having the improved life from infancy, Venerable, you showed yourself to be a skilled priest and followed Saint Calinic with faith and piety. Therefore, be our helper and intercessor to the Lord so that we may find mercy and grace from Him and sing to you with joy:

Rejoice, blessed priest under the burning candle;
Rejoice, Father of those seeking divine adoption;
Rejoice, spiritual vision of the mysteries of the Kingdom;
Rejoice, consciousness of wonderful discoveries;
Rejoice, unceasing worship, gate to heaven;

Rejoice, light-bearing torch of the Church;
Rejoice, helper of the priests of Christ;
Rejoice, protector of monks and nuns in temptations and persecutions;
Rejoice, burning torch for the faithful;
Rejoice, for in humility you have reached the likeness of the Savior Christ;
Rejoice, for, in your running, you have reached the reward of the calling from above;
Rejoice, pleasing sacrifice received by God;
Rejoice, Holy Father Irodion, made wise by God!

**Kontakion 9**

Father, being worthy to stand before the Throne of divinity, we beseech you to pour out grace from heaven upon us, so that through your word, God Himself may speak and we may shout with joy: Alleluia!

**Ikos 9**

You enlightened the hermits like a star, and with the deeds of faith, you shone on earth, spending time with the angels, Father. And for the faith of the Gospel, you gathered them all in one spirit, advising them to live worthily, Reverend, for this, we sing to you:
Rejoice, flower of ascetic labors;
Rejoice, encouragement towards struggles of the laity;
Rejoice, vigil in prayer with the groups of monks;
Rejoice, thanksgiving brought in the name of the Lord with the council of priests;
Rejoice, knowledge beyond knowledge of God's love;
Rejoice, disciple's obedience before the priests;
Rejoice, for you have crucified your body with your passions and desires;
Rejoice, for you have resembled in the Spirit the great Fathers of the Church;
Rejoice, for you have gained the reward of heavenly life with them;

Rejoice, son and heir of the Kingdom of God;
Rejoice, Father, through whom Christ takes form in those called by Him;
Rejoice, recipient of the promise of the Holy Spirit through faith;
Rejoice, Holy Father Irodion, made wise by God!

**Kontakion 10**

Father, through fasting and prayer, you expelled the enemy's work from your soul and body, taking from God a powerful word. Therefore, the multitudes of people, receiving healing from your grace, gratefully shouted: Alleluia!

**Ikos 10**

Revealing yourself as an angel in the flesh, you accepted to live as a hermit in the Lainici Monastery, blessed Father. And with the power of faith overcoming the passions, you gathered many believers around you, who glorified God, singing:
Rejoice, mighty speaker of the Holy Spirit;
Rejoice, consolation of love and peace from above;
Rejoice, for you embrace all with a holy embrace;
Rejoice, fruitful thought towards the obedience of Christ;
Rejoice, for you have become rich with the poverty of the embodied Son of God;
Rejoice, repentance unto salvation, without remorse;
Rejoice, new creature in the Lord;
Rejoice, purity of spiritual love;
Rejoice, bodily bearer of Christ's crucifixion;
Rejoice, body in which the life of Christ the Savior was revealed;
Rejoice, soul ruled by the love of the Most Holy Trinity;
Rejoice, for you have renewed yourself spiritually, climbing from step to step;
Rejoice, Holy Father Irodion, made wise by God!

## Kontakion 11

Feeling your end near, the brothers gathered to listen to your last encouragement. So, seeing in spirit the last of them, you said to them: 'Let us sit well, let us sit fearfully and remember the holy sacrifice, which we will offer in peace, singing: Alleluia!'

## Ikos 11

Blessed Irodion, your spirit had ascended to heaven with the angels, but your body was an unspoiled treasure forever for healing our souls and bodies. That is why all the faithful sing to you:
Rejoice, seer of God's mysteries;
Rejoice, consolation of monks and Christians;
Rejoice, circumcision of the heart in the spirit;
Rejoice, fruit for sanctification;
Rejoice, ministry for the renewal of the Spirit;
Rejoice, suffering together with Christ;
Rejoice, glory with Him;
Rejoice, altar of the name of Jesus;
Rejoice, victor over evil through good deeds;
Rejoice, for you have rested in the fulfillment of the divine will;
Rejoice, speaker in words learned from the Holy Spirit;
Rejoice, worker with God;
Rejoice, Holy Father Irodion, made wise by God!

## Kontakion 12

Praying to the Mother of God, you held to your chest the Cross of the Savior Christ and you gave your spirit into the hands of the Master, leaving us your body full of holiness that heals diseases and unbinds untied bonds, for the communion of those who sing: Alleluia!

## Ikos 12

Today, the whole community of hermits gathers at the grace from above and celebrates Saint Irodion at the Master's feast, glorifying

his honorable sleep and joyfully singing:
Rejoice, entrance into the joy of the Lord;
Rejoice, abode of the Most Holy Trinity;
Rejoice, body clothed in immortality;
Rejoice, change from glory to glory;
Rejoice, perfect love that banishes fear;
Rejoice, partaker of the divine nature;
Rejoice, communion of the holiness of Christ the Savior;
Rejoice, blameless vigil to the Lord's coming;
Rejoice, mercy to the hopeless world;
Rejoice, name written in the book of life;
Rejoice, blessed rest in the spirit of stillness;
Rejoice, image made an icon of perpetual worship;
Rejoice, Holy Father Irodion, made wise by God!

**Kontakion 13**

O Reverend Father Irodion, great servant of God's grace, receive this little prayer from us and bring it to the Throne of the Most Holy Trinity so that we can be delivered from all troubles and sufferings and sing to you: Alleluia! (Repeat this kontakion three times.)

Repeat Ikos 1 and Kontakion 1.

**Ikos 1**

The great Hierarch Calinic of Cernica chose you as a spiritual father, Venerable Irodion, and appointed you the advisor of the monks; for, in your youth, he saw the perfection of your pious life, for which we cry out to you:

Rejoice, morning star of Lainici;
Rejoice, good shepherd;
Rejoice, for you have communed from the chalice of eternity;
Rejoice, heart of a father and maker of sons of light;
Rejoice, son of the Oltean land, received as a brother in Cernica;
Rejoice, for you have become a great abbot in the Lainici Monastery;

Rejoice, for many disciples you gave birth to in the Holy Spirit here;
Rejoice, vessel of the gift before the sight;
Rejoice, long-suffering bearer of the cross;
Rejoice, supporter of the helpless;
Rejoice, liberation by the grace of the enslaved creation;
Rejoice, word with divine fruition;
Rejoice, Holy Father Irodion, made wise by God!

**Kontakion 1**

Let us all praise the morning star from Lainici, Irodion, the one with an Apostle name; for he, having become a skilled priest, the shepherd of Oltenia, showed himself to be brilliant, and in the mountain, he multiplied his disciples, who called out to him: Rejoice, Holy Father Irodion, made wise by God!

## Biography

Saint Irodion was born in 1821 in Bucharest and received the name John at baptism. His parents gave him good education and taught him Christian behaviour ever since he was a child.

At that time, at Cernica Monastery, nearby Bucharest, under the guidance of Saint abbot George, disciple of Saint Paisios from Neamţ, the spiritual work of prayer and obedience was growing, work which would be continued by Saint abbot Callinicus, the future bishop of Râmnic.

Having heard of the fame of the spiritual life over there, young John, aged 22, asked for the blessing of his bodily parents and retired to Cernica Monastery, under the guidance of abbot Callinicus. There, the young novice was submitted to various trials and soon he passed through all forms of obedience, courageously resisting to all temptations.

Blessed John slept only three or four hours at night and spent all the rest of his time in prayer and prostrations. He was present at all the services in the church, which he attended with much spiritual joy, his lips always saying the prayer: "Jesus Christ, Son of God, have mercy on me, the sinner".

In 1846, he was tonsured into monasticism with the name of Irodion and ordained deacon and, soon after, priest, according to the decision of his abbot Saint Callinicus. After ordination, blessed hieromonk Irodion fasted, prayed and made prostrations more than before, so that his new quality as a priest did not change anything in his way of living; on the contrary, made him even more humble towards all those around.

In 1850, following the insistence of ruler prince Barbu Ştirbei, Saint abbot Callinicus accepted to be bishop to the Eparchy of Râmnic. The worthy abbot shed many tears when he left the community of Cernica Monastery and took a few fathers with him to help him with the administration of the Diocese of Râmnic. One of those who accompanied him was Venerable Irodion, whom he appointed ecclesiarch at Lainici Skete, in 1851, when he also made him protosyncelos. Soon after that, Saint Callinicus would appoint protosyncelos Irodion igumen of this skete, where he would remain until the end of his life.

As soon as Venerable Irodion became igumen, he increased even greater the trials with more endeavour. For him, the greater responsibility to God and people, the greater endeavour had to be. Having seen Irodion's thought and efforts, God bestowed great spiritual gifts into his heart. But the devil, the permanent enemy of the humankind, could not put up with the humbleness and spiritual efforts of Venerable Irodion, so that he hit him with his poisonous arrows.

Thus, that enemy entered into the hearts of some monastic brothers and brought to the blessed Irodion much bitterness. Some lay people came together with those rebels, successors of the founders of the skete, who were eager to rule the monastic community as they wished. Consequently, Venerable Irodion has been removed from leading that community for a while. But, being called back, God has blessed him with numerous spiritual gifts.

Soon, administrated by Venerable Irodion, Lainici Skete had gathered the biggest monastic community of Oltenia, exceeding even bigger and older monasteries. His fame was greater and greater so that when the father confessor of Saint Hierarch Callinicus, Bishop of Râmnic, died he decided to take Venerable Irodion as his spiritual father, although he was much younger than him and had been his disciple.

The gift of Father Irodion was really great because all those who came to him could find peace for their souls and hearts, healing of diseases and casting out bad spirits. Venerable Irodion lived an even stricter life and God bestowed even greater and richer gifts upon him, so that he came to foreknow what would happen. Given all the virtues Venerable Irodion had, Saint Hierarch Callinicus called him the "Morning Star from Lainici", because he guided and advised many people on the path to salvation just like a star in the sky.

As a monk, his heart and mind were directed to heaven, but as abbot he took good care of the fathers and brethren of the monastery whom he protected from temptations and devilish attacks.

Saint Irodion performed a great act of love for his nation in 1877, when he sent 12 brothers from his monastery as health workers to look after the sick and injured in the War of Independence. He has also shown great love for the lay faithful in need, sending relief aid to the poor and hungry.

Venerable Irodion passed away on 3 May 1900. His relics were found on 10 April 2009 and laid at Lainici Monastery for veneration, where they can still be seen today.

On 29 October 2010, the Holy Synod of the Romanian Orthodox Church placed him among saints, being celebrated on 3 May.

Through his holy prayers, Lord Jesus Christ, our God, have mercy on us. Amen.

**Books published by Nun Christina Oceanitissa:**

The collective works of St Nektarios of Aegina.
The Philokalia 5: The full text in English.
The collective works of Elder Cleopa.
The Anacreontic Poems by Saint Sophronius Patriarch of Jerusalem.
The Life of Saint Paul of Thebes the First Hermit.
The Devil: The Cause of Sin by Saint John of Kronstadt.
Faith and the Orthodox Church by Saint John of Kronstadt.
The Monastic Rule of Saint Pachomius the Great.
Supplicatory Canon and Akathist to St Paisios.
Supplicatory Canon and Akathist to St Porphyrios.
Supplicatory Canon and Akathist to St George.
Supplicatory Canon and Akathist to St Anastasia.
Supplicatory Canon and Akathist to St Anna.
Supplicatory Canon and Akathist to St John the Russian.
Supplicatory Canon and Akathist to St Ephraim of Nea Makri.
Supplicatory Canon and Akathist to St John Maximovitch.
Supplicatory Canon and Akathist to St Dimitri.
Supplicatory Canon and Akathist to St Joseph the Hesycast.
Supplicatory Canon and Akathist to St Luke the Surgeon.
Supplicatory Canon and Akathist to St John the Baptist.
The Way of a Pilgrim.
Conversation with a Grieving Man by St Dimitri of Rostov.
The Inner Man by St Dimitri of Rostov.
Orthodox Prayer Book.
Daily Orthodox Prayer book.

www.ingramcontent.com/pod-product-compliance
Lightning Source LLC
LaVergne TN
LVHW010512160826
845677LV00012B/2814

* 9 7 9 8 8 4 8 9 1 9 6 3 9 *